KISS

POLLY CLARK

Kiss

To Lilly
Best wishes
Polly Clark

BLOODAXE BOOKS

ISBN: 1 85224 535 2

First published 2000 by
Bloodaxe Books Ltd,
Highgreen,
Tarset,
Northumberland NE48 1RP.

Second impression 2004.

www.bloodaxebooks.com
For further information about Bloodaxe titles
please visit our website or write to
the above address for a catalogue.

Bloodaxe Books Ltd acknowledges
the financial assistance of
Arts Council England, North East.

Printed in Great Britain by
Cromwell Press Ltd, Trowbridge, Wiltshire.

Acknowledgements

Acknowledgements are due to the editors of the following publications in which some of these poems, or versions of them, first appeared: *Envoi, Iota, New Blood* (Bloodaxe Books 1999), *Orbis, Oxford Poetry, Poetry London, The Rialto, The Richmond Review, Singularities: Three Eric Gregory Award Winners* (Hubble, 1997), *Stand, Staple, The Tabla Book of New Verse* and *Thumbscrew*. 'Bears' was commissioned by Oxford University Press for their English language teaching course, *Network*.

For their insight and criticism I am grateful to Matthew Hollis and the John Florio Society at Magdalen College.

I would like to thank the Society of Authors for an Eric Gregory Award in 1997.

Contents

Love Story

You winked at me in the hospital chrome,
and turning in my sheets I found
the imprints of your lips and feet.
When darkness fell, the young girl opposite
was alone and began to cry,
I went to stroke her hair
and you returned to me, you were

the swarthy nurse in green
whose sole job was to lift girls
from bed to trolley and back again.
My arms around your neck,
I whispered, 'Nagyon erős',
it meant 'I love you', it meant don't leave me,
let me bury myself in your green cloth,
let me be such a clean thing.

And I saw you in the green waist
of my father, the surgeon, whose hand
reached from the sky to my face,
and said in a dream language,
God is waiting at the door
and will go if you ask. I watched
you leave me in the gleam of the needle
and I heard your pipe in the distance
and the anxious footsteps of daylight
pattering over me like children.

Snow

Your words are falling on me,
not one at a time, but in half-words,
in soft phrases, the exquisite *fizz*!
of a single letter on my tongue.
I walk home in a blizzard
of everything you have said to me;

and not only words, your touch
babbles warmly on my skin; syllable
by syllable you're obliterating
the dark needles of the fir trees; a crow
is trying to scythe himself free
of the fragments cohering
into one great white word.

Letter from Pécs

This is my day: I put out milk for
the enormous winter-coloured tom,
who avalanches on my bed, out-staring me
with metal eyes, and I enclose your absence
in thick wool and a jacket,
running from my whitewashed cell into
the giant's windswept garden;

and now the nights are swallowing the mornings
as though the sun should never
have escaped at all; this winter everything
is sharpened: leaves and rooftops and
my breathing slicing
shapes out of the sky.

In a hole, somewhere, is a huge rusted key,
heavy with discovery by generations of children.
The tom knows where it is
(that's why I humour him), I think
he dragged it there, I think that everybody knows.
The gibbering people who inhabit this garden
will never tell me, sometimes I feel
I am a speck on their teeth, compressed
between their jolting lips, or
shivering on the whites of their eyes.

When my eyes open onto
this iron sheet of dawn, my heart
is dead and silver, frozen and beautiful like a snowflake.
When night opens its mouth
I throw it, high above the hunchbacked wall;
if you look tonight
you will see it, round and hoping,
looking for a place to fall.

Brief Encounter

I never knew you, though
I wrote page upon page about
how you would feel inside my heart
and in my pen, and how
my life would be corrected
by the ballast of you in my gut. But
I never saw you, though I searched –
in the eye-whites of the gypsy, in
the smiles of people who never asked anything of me,
in traces of blood, flakes of skin,
one long curling hair which lay between
my pages. They all made words line up neatly in my mind,
but where were you? My authenticity,
the soul of everything I meant to say,
where were you, I never knew you.
Until today. I stood beneath the hot stream
of water, washing away my headache and hatred
for hour after hour, and then, in a drop on my eyelash,
I saw you move, I saw you move! I saw
your shiny black carapace
shrinking beneath hot tears of water
and your fat black legs
lumbering to safety. It was not what I imagined,
grief. Nor the convulsive reaction,
the terror, the urge to survive,
the roaring and stamping in my head,
the smell of heat and hallucinations, the voices,
bury the dead, bury the dead.

Waiter

Keleti Station, Budapest

You nod your four words of English,
patiently repeat my order,
my head spins with fatigue and coffee.

Sharp and practised as a seal,
you bring and retrieve. Behind you
jumbled bottles slowly dull,
· cream-cakes age quietly.

I have nearly an hour to kill,
so I like you, you smile behind your clean glasses,
your badly hemmed waistcoat
looks jaunty, decadent.
Through the slats between the syllables
we peer cautiously, invited.

Road to Chisholm

Climbing the road to Chisholm, with
the mist weeping on the car, my grandmother
staring at a memory lost
in the verdant muddy verge, I saw
a galloping horse in the valley, orange
against the humbled green and the grey
mist-balls of sheep, galloping
calmly, like a film-horse.
We climbed until I almost saw
the stillness of its back.
No one saw it but me. No one spoke, not liking
to interrupt the steady command of the wipers
or fight the protests of the rain drawn
beneath the tyres. In this silence I followed it.
Who turned it loose in such a huge place,
who left it in the rain,
who knew what I knew, that love had left us,
and this was all we had,
the rain, our bodies, a destination.

Retribution

Snow, exploded stone,
a chance to be air
taken brutally −

coughing I raise myself,
wolf-backed, ape-handed,

like the girl I saw kicked to the floor,
who got up six times
and kept on walking,
eyes fixed beyond despair.

In my face
explodes the sky, expelling me;
unhappy excrement,
smother it, kick it,
the boy in boots has made his judgement.

The boy in boots
crashed his motorbike later,
impaled himself on railings.
I knew it was retribution.
I took his inarticulate hate
and made it my own.

Adultery

Water the plant every day, you say.
Taking it I cannot make our hands touch,

for I will still want you when you are old,
when memories and guilt make us cry,

when your loose-limbed frame of memories
bends its thin arms around me.

Our old old stories, we turn them over
like photos on the two-seater sofa;

the others sit quietly, strangely
tolerant of this love-making, this

non-contact of knees, averting of eyes,
banalities opened into like kisses.

We are numbed with shame, we converse
over and around it, the wordless please.

Zoo

I remember kicking the bales down
from the top of the barn, my eyes streaming.

The only creature I truly loved
hugged me, and I thought his animal warmth

was more wonderful than the touch on my cheek
from the gibbon with the circular brown eyes.

The orang-utan liked to scrub with a rag
and poke her leathery fingers through the bars,

and the elephant stood at the railings, curling
her trunk at the children,

her ears like rags, and her tusks
wrenched out; I thought

suffering must have a language, I loved
where love was wasted.

When the silly pop-eyed Père David
escaped across the zebras' frozen savannah

he chased it and threw
his great shoulders at its hooves

bringing it down in a trembling
thump, and I thought the breaking

of freedom was beautiful, I thought
I was discovering truth

in these limbs collapsing,
antlers falling against the sky,

and the snow in shreds
like a man's blue eye.

When You Were Made

I think God was uncertain
when he dressed you in blue

and yanked your back up straight
and filled your eyes with ink,

made clumsy pens of your lips,
a blank page of your skin;

he was uncertain of your power,
could this bony thing, scribbling

poems and always alone
be a force to be reckoned with?

But still proud he sealed
your funny frame with a kiss,

carved you a perfect white shoulder
from Sirius.

Your Blue Shirt

today's sun is turning to yesterday's
all around us, and the road is rolling
in blue, and I've forgotten about
crying because we're laughing,

for these wheels belong to me, and this
sky belongs to me, and sun pours
over my wrists like a beautiful scarf,
and you're smiling from somewhere inside you –

and then the tarmac smacks my ribs,
and the bike has long gone,
and your blue shirt
rolls from me like a scrap of sky,

and pain blooms in my temple,
and dark blood has broken onto my hands,
and people are running towards us like children
across half-remembered fields, in white sun.

If You're Interested

you're very talented my
favourites no girl
I ever knew before could
if you're interested
if you're interested
tarantino's women are all
running I'm getting a belly you'll
do brilliantly I'll see
you next week sometime shall I
break his legs for you? if you're
starving and I lost but I'm not
grumpy fantastic-looking
slim-wise, my favourites, if
you're easier to stop
now than later, if you're
sorry I'm trying to do the right
thing sorry I upset you sorry
I make you if you're interested
my favourites are running tonight

Pilgrimage

Across a clifftop stretched our shadows,
yours before you, mine behind you,

a pilgrimage over salty grass
to where the sun blazed the distant backs of seals.

The icy sea and track half-starved
whispered *it is never over*

and the overflowing sun
swept away my name.

We turned and saw a huge black dog
pound its way from a break in the earth,

to circle its master, barking.

Where Swans Have Lain Down

Here where swans have lain down
lain down among the rushes,

like crinolines blown in the rushes
where light decays on the water,

leaving lines in fallen leaves
where flies unpunctuate the evening;

here where leaves like pages fall,
where ripples circle the drinking light,

a bird calls, clear as a name,
alone in the place where swans have lain down.

In the Pool Room

Under the lemony light,
my paw resting on the green baize,

his lion's mouth presses
a kiss like a roar into me.

Paws flounder into manes,
mouths break and seal,

and my throat bends like a belly,
while blue eyes blink in flat faces

and tails flicker round us.
Then it is over

like a shiver over sleeping ribs,
and I lick my lips,

like a young cub
digesting its first lesson.

South Uist

In the morning the track paled
to fit only two feet pressing down
to the proud wreckage at the sea's breast.

All the long night I lay in your damp bed,
felt how the sheets that wrapped you
loved me less, breaking the hours

with sips of peat-treacled water.
I dreamed of you as dawn
flooded over the dry stone walls.

I never spoke of it. I broke instead
the bull's skull from its armoury of shells,
dragged it home, to bleach away its shadows.

Last Tango in the Men's Department

Shoulders stacked in cellophane,
pockets smell of hurt unborn,
of black, brown and blue,
the whirl of a bruise.

Mannequin girls tilt their heads
as they press the dark cashmere
hand to heart; I hold
the navy like a stranger I rescued,

beautiful creature,
I know the size of your shoe,
I know all about you,
how rooms sweep around you.

I spin as the lady
counts the rings of your neck,
your throat so close
she could scratch it or kiss it –

your trust is amazing,
but you can't hear the music:
the sadness of shoulders bent over knees,
the anger of metal lifted and swung,

the swirl of a dress
like a bloom blown in,
the break of the doors,
the thump of the sun.

My Life with Horses

Before I knew there were men,
I galloped a pony bareback;
it was a hard winter, but
how sure-footed we were, resolute
in frozen emptiness, stamping
the ice with our names.

Years later I lay like a foal in the grass,
wanting to touch your hair;
we clutched like shadows,
I twined the past through my fingers, kissing
great gulps of father, of mother,
galloping, with nothing to stop me.

Now in the evening I put on my dress
like a secret; will you see
how my elbow pokes like a hock,
the way I have carefully cut my mane,
the way my eyes roll from fear of you?
I'm trying to hide the animal I am;

and you give me a necklace,
bright as a bit, and you're
stamping your name
into the earth, and my arm
is around you, weak as a halter,
and nothing can stop me, no mother or father.

A Lunch Date with My Father

As you're speaking I'm dreaming
of leaning over the pizza
of leaning over the salad
of leaning over to stop with a kiss
the sun crashing through the window
like a lion with huge paws.
My father's eyes are black as a canopy,
my father's lip is hard as a tusk,
my father's heart is a broken river;
beside my father I feel like a vulture.
Later we embrace like cubs,
whose parents are gone, lost in the sun.

Take-off

We are rocketing through layers of feeling
to a place that does not feel;
at 10,000 feet I watch the clouds restlessly
impress their frail dreams upon one another;
and though I think of you, you are no more real
than these mouths roaring and dissolving beneath me.
I grow emptier but the plane powers on;
I am leaving everything, leaving you,
like a hat suddenly spiralling up,
to where strangers kiss and death is gone,
and streamers soar in white and blue.

My Mother Marries My Father

Stitching her neat white wedding hem
I say, *this is how it happens,*
people pull hardest where there is least love.
My mother looks at me through violet eyes,
you don't understand anything.

Years later I trawl my father
from the ocean of the past
and ask him, did you love her?
His answer is to kiss me on the lips,
his answer is to say, *I've nothing to hide,*
his answer is to watch me
like a fisherman watches a fish out of water,
mourning something, behind blank eyes.

When I Close My Eyes

When I close my eyes,
the rain pours, like
rain on a foreign window;

your body is soft
and awkward, as if grief
is finally over;

I hold you like
a survivor, I hold your flesh
like warm sand;

when I close my eyes
the words pour like rain
pouring for the first time.

Excitement

The day has blinked, the streets are awash with blue
the mood of God is lonely;
all day he sent his frozen grief away, unfettered
it swirled and tumbled, unaware of falling.
All day I've waited on the inside,
watching the light grow fat and fade away.
God doesn't know of my excitement,
look my hands are neatly folded.
God doesn't know I've been possessed,
look I'm bright and smartly dressed.
But my heart's a lump of you,
I'm an empty bed at empty noon;
I'm a stone wall smacked with sunlight,
I'm a stick of rock with KISS stamped through.

Flowers

I hold them like the wrist
of a troublesome child,
I drop them in a bag.
Still trying to touch me, they say
we are like the foreign country
you left but still carry
in a book of photographs;
they think I'm sentimental,
that the dreams I had mean something to me,
that one day I won't be able to do this.

A man cut from the future
is waiting for me in the rain.
The walls are undressed
and left like a child,
the past is tucked for transit
in its familiar box. Later I ask him
did you know I would find you?
am I no longer alone?
He kisses me among the selves
that never made it this far.

Walk in the Rain

You walk for miles beside me
through trees that open out too quickly
onto rain-soaked common land.
I tell you almost everything,
I feel it coming out of me, like a sickness.
And you sit beside me
on a bench sodden with rain and the smell of things over
and you're telling me all those things are over,
and you're kissing me because they're all over,
and our bodies drift like leaves on the water,
and the people in the distance are made of water,
and the lake is swallowing, with a million mouths a second,
all the things I ever wanted, all the things that are over.

New Forest Ponies

Here come the ponies
down the gutted track,
with old women's chins,
biting for apples, scalloping
the earth with their beggars' legs.
I call to them, my hands
dark as soft apples.

Their warmth is sharper than fire,
their smell licks round me,
hooves crack like twigs;

you're in the car, uneasy
as the ponies clatter noiselessly.
They're coming at me, with their
anger all messy in their hearts.
They're circling me softly
like a body dragged from leaves,
my discarded, hungry dreams
come to find me.

Sunset

I watched the sun roll
down the nape of the hill
like a great ball caught by Atlas.

I watched the most perfect gold coin
fall from a careless palm
into nothingness, and all the people

seemed to be standing in rags
at the edge of a biblical flood.
But to the girls on bikes

dodging the rocks in the path and laughing,
to the beautiful girl with
sandstone lips and a terrier called Max,

to the couples with their children,
the dropping of the sun
like the corner of space melting

was nothing to be remarked on;
no more than if you
had looked up from among the swans,

and when I did not move
had crossed the bridge towards me.
Mothers running to their daughters

are a commonplace, and the sun of
unimaginable red, rolling away
and turning the water to death

and the grass to flesh,
leaving the world with no promises,
is a commonplace.

Amsterdam

Here in Amsterdam the homes
dam the flooding sky
with open sleepy eyes, dreaming
of ordinary things.

My hand in yours in the black and green
of a searing winter;
on the cobbles bikes bounce,
faces stare steadfastly ahead;

we sip tiny beers, we talk of gaps in love;
please don't say it's us. Above
the glowing streets, we make love
to foreign sounds, familiar touches;

and later in a blue corner
of the Bourbon, a man
as tall as my father,
with hair twice as white

is speaking inflected English.
He has the stoop of someone
plucked out of love; he has
hands that let his children fall;

and in the heart of Amsterdam
a woman's mouth is open,
and a man is forgetting who she is,
I can feel him forgetting her

in the floor sobbing the blues,
in the jumbled bodies hammering
their weakness, their fury,
into all hope, into a spine of stairs.

How to Love You

With my body?
You can pick that up anywhere:
the top shelf of the newsagent's,
or teasingly obscured in brown paper
where we stop for sweets.
There's nothing special about its
hotchpotch of dark and light,
named, scored, hotly debated.
A long time ago, this hand-me-down body
scored an almost perfect 9.9,
when winter's ice had given me an edge
and the world fell away for an instant,
and I was nothing, and he was nothing too,
and the world was a place where bodies were new as snow.
But that's the kind of thing I'd make up,
the kind of dream I'd embellish for a touch
from a world warmly dressed,
strangely kind to my nakedness;
and so, I don't know how to love you.
With my heart? I believe you know
the heart's full of unknowable blood.
It's no place for you.

The Passerby

Today, though not in a hurry
(only remembering how it was
that my father seemed to break
the light around him, could not fit into it)

I passed a wolfish boy or man
cluttered in the street, splashed
aside by the rain of feet
around him on his slab of space.

Spare any change was what he said to me
in his dirtied words churned out,
not-really words, for not-really me
and though not in a hurry,

I didn't even murmur *sorry*,
I rained past him and over him,
or at least over his shape
battered dark like a rock.

Reader, I scrambled over him
like the horrified child of my father
who simply has to get somewhere,
somewhere abandonment cannot get to,

somewhere cruelty cannot reach.

Szechèny Tér

I *The Consultant*

The consultant was draped in white
as if to protect himself from dust
in a great abandoned house.
To the round-faced Hungarian woman he spoke,
who spoke in French to my French friend,
who translated brokenly to me.
In a small polite line we stood
beneath this mountainous man
whose face I dared not look into.
Tell him, I hissed up the line, *tell him
if he doesn't do it, I'll do it myself.*
It was as if I'd been left on a frozen hillside
and having unexpectedly survived
was then brought in to meet my maker.
I was trembling so hard I could hardly speak,
my lips were heavy and blue,
conversation screamed around me,
drenching me as though in snow.
What is he saying? I whispered, but no one answered.
The consultant had a chest so deep and wide
I might have clambered up on it to die.
It seemed as good a place as any, a place
as indifferent and clean as any.
Then they were filing me out,
someone mad, held together
just by women's hands.
What is he saying? I said,
or maybe I said nothing
as they led me away.

II *The Angels*

We were robed in white like angels.
We were taken downwards.
The others would not look at me.

They muttered their spiky language.
Their mothers in their reds and browns
huddled to them like huge birds,

their eyes hard and pale
like beautiful foreign pebbles,
or the painted eyes of the chapel's Mary.

When the doors opened,
nurses like mountain faces
came to take us.

They washed us,
they dressed us,
they stood us in line.

A silent chorus of white
to be wheeled
one by one

into quiet arms
that drained the light from the room
and the fear from us,

sending us out flat as paper,
slack-mouthed and open-wristed,
white robe in disarray,

and rows of angels lifting their heads,
observing without pity
this new bloom of ugly red.

III *The Wish*

I never thought it would hurt me,
but as it found a place
to cling to inside me,
like an almost invisible tern
latching itself to the cliffside,
and all you see is the flash
of unnatural blue when the storm
changes its direction –
as it found somewhere,
it dug in and I cried out.
I knew then. I knew before
I began to lie awake all night
and cook up pasta at 3 a.m.,
before your postcard arrived
coffee-splashed and bright from Idaho,
before the summer burned
itself out, became a shell
through which the winter tore.
It grew colder and colder,
my breasts began to weep.
Stepping out onto the ice, I whispered
I wish I wish I wish
but there was no sound from anywhere.
The ice was thick as oil.
I let myself slide
down the corkscrew road,
down, into a strange drowning,
and in its reflection I saw what was inside me,
pale-faced, small, with no comprehensible wish.

IV *The Dream*

I can't find the hospital
and each morning that I can't find the hospital,
the old woman stands in the February glare
of Szechèny Tér and holds out
a bunch of snowdrops, doubling
its price just for me.

Szalon Sör

At first we devoured it,
at 30p, so astoundingly *cheap*,
dark brown and sweet,
its smell whorling into the air from the sör gyár.
Americans wouldn't touch it,
so goddamn *thick* they complained,
while the locals leant round bottles of it,
their child-tummied bodies
packing the tiny söröző,
their hard laughter
clattering out into the dusty street.

Years on, we've come back
to find most things more faded still,
except the labels on the Szalon
which now show a king with his glass raised,
and horsemen galloping in to crush the Turks,
and with glasses to match,
embossed in brilliant red and gold.
We are thrilled, we barter excitedly
and take a set from the waiter for 500 forints.
We give them pride of place in our living-rooms,
stack our best pens in them.

Stephen Selects the Photographs

Stephen's hands are the washed out
magnolia of an old rented room,
his eyes are bleached from years
of striplight through film;

through his soft shirt, slightly open,
his body is thin like a girl-model's,
his shoulders jut as he leans
forensically

into an ordered world of technical detail.
Is it *nice*? Is it *pink*? is it?
Is it *neat*? And somewhere, even far away, is she *smiling*?
It is long ago, I am numbed to the wonder

that a body so slight, so
appealingly slight, can observe another so,
and feel no kinship, no pity,
no welling of tears, nor surprise that it is so.

These are strange facts to possess:
how a naked body lies
as if sorry in the hands,
how flesh breaks namelessly open. Facts like this

aren't mine. Mine are the lowered eyes
as wearily you squint through slide after slide,
a quietly disgusted Aryan soldier
whose fingertip indicates this way or that.

I found you kind back then,
I thought my prayers were love-songs
muttered in the street
and in the arms of men,

may you always find me *nice*
let me be not *slag* or *dog*
may I never make you angry
may you never turn on me.

Letter to the Man I Love

When feeling cheated, remember
that you are loved
by the only one who didn't cry.
This may seem small consolation,
and perhaps you would prefer
that you were not loved by
someone of such monumental achievement.
Please, let me explain.
I have watched as people are stripped naked
and made to writhe on the floor.
I do not know them, nor
what they may have done to deserve this.
I have, however, invented names for them, and stories
about how much they enjoy it.
I have filled their mouths with lies,
and I have answered letters from the general public
as if I were them, repeating those lies.
I have written their confessions
which were totally untrue
and received payment for the forgery.
I have given, on request,
photos of them in various poses to friends
and even to my own father (who was delighted)
in order to make myself more popular (which it did).
I have, on social occasions, announced
that my varied tasks I find 'liberating',
and on that basis have found myself,
on more than one occasion
embodying those lies.
I have answered phone calls from the general public
who wish to know in *exactly* what way
I would like to be stripped
and pushed to the floor,
with scrupulous politeness,
following the company code that all callers are customers.
I have not, until now,
questioned out loud

the glaring fact that all these people
stripped and lied about
are not unlike myself, and that I
have written about them as if they were dogs or mice
because that is the only way to lie about them convincingly.
Nor have I, until today,
when I couldn't stop crying,
realised the impossibility of love
with someone to whom
I have lied so much.

My Education at the Zoo

There is a rule which I am born knowing,
from the moment I slip out, and my mouth

becomes that anguished, red, newborn hole,
its ridge of unborn teeth uselessly bared.

I know this rule and am flailing against it.
But in later years I come to an uneasy acceptance;

my unusual physical strength is a testament
to its weight. When I am 16

I can push a barrow overflowing
with rolling cow haunch and pony carcass

all the way up the hill to the wolves.
Only the strongest of the strong men can do it:

there is laughter, and something else, a recognition.
On New Year's Eve, when one year metamorphoses

into a dream of another, they kiss me
with uneasy, snarling kisses.

The Amazon parrot whirls at me,
a green screech as I approach his nest;

next door, the cockatoo is pacing up and down,
he clambers up me, as if I were a gnarled tropical tree,

lodges his head down my shirt between my breasts,
murmurs (you must incline your head to hear his words)

fuck you bitch, his yellow eyes blinking.
I'm afraid at the end I begin to fall apart,

and accidentally set three pairs of lovebirds free
and the cockatoo, who simply climbs the nearest tree

and hurls insults (but suddenly the words begin to come,
secretly, when I am alone at night).

The real men bask at lunchtime, like lions keeping
their violence to themselves while the sun is hot.

At night, at party after party, I find it hard
to keep from being discovered or blurting the truth.

I drink ten pints, laugh at all insults,
refuse to retreat, as finally amidst howls

of laughter at 3 a.m., one of them emerges
wearing two bras and a nightie, his face covered in paint,

and everyone cheering his victory in the game
that he is playing, that now I know the name of.

The Pet Rabbit

I can't call it love, I call it *white*,
a slash of rock, a touchable sky,
colourless, but swallowing light
with hollowed out hands and mis-shapen eye,
stooping to smell me and whispering *my*
as it scoops me up from the muddied rain,
mumbling dumbly, an attempt to explain

its need of me, its fear of being alone,
for which I am the talisman, a familiar black,
set in a box like a glittering stone
where it nourishes me as though I were its lack,
bringing fragments of life, holding a universe back,
and at the end of the day taking sound and all light
to an easier sleep, to a dream-filled night.

The Foot-soldier

As though I would survive,
I forgave the digging of my body
in preparation for war.
I had my basic training,

I clutched my rations to me
and counted them at night.
At dawn I pushed aside the corpses
and went over the top.

I stumbled through no man's land,
living miracle after miracle,
that I could still hurt, that I still lived,
that I might reach the other side.

They gave me a badge and an office
and I ignored the devastation,
the bodies upright as though neatly shot,
the corpses guzzling in their suits,

the long corridors all leading to loss,
the empty screens crackling against my fingers.
As though I would survive
I *became good*, I *learned to love*.

At night I curled and dreamed
I was alive. By day I neatly filed
my names away, ticking as appropriate
squandered, stolen, marched away at gunpoint.

Dora

In 1900 Sigmund Freud treated 'Dora', a girl of 18, for what was at that time termed hysteria. His analysis concluded that it was her repressed desires that had caused her symptoms.

There's a lot wrong with me.
Saying it makes me ugly.
I don't know how to say it, I
don't know how to say
what has happened to me.

Alone, I try not to remember.
The truth has shaped itself into a parody of me,
curled up in me like a baby,
a sinful ugly baby
that cannot be loved, nor delivered.

The truth has no words.
Without words there can be no "facts".
And Dr Freud wants facts from me.
Tell me what happened, he says. I offer him
my stumbling, manacled dreams.

He says I'm in love with Herr K.
He says I'm in love with Frau K.
He says I'm in love with my father.
He says I'm probably in love with him.
Can't he see what happens

when words confront the truth?
They scatter like rats.
They become non-words, non-sense.
I am dulled, as if a long stoning
finally is ending.

If I yield, he promises
there will be comfort.
I would like to be comforted.
Sir, we will do without the truth
we will do without it –

excuse my breathlessness as I stand,
my unsteadiness, my ugly limp. My body,
unruly thing, still tries you see
to say it, to push it out of me,
what happened to me.

Crime of Passion

The cow is the good woman,
the woman we'd like to be.
The cow dips her blunt lips
into the slow river.
She's sleek, she eats well;
her udder, heart of her cowishness,
sways like a pleasant mushroom she's quietly cultivating.
The cow is never angry.
She wears her yellow tag indifferently,
like an heirloom she's too young to know the meaning of.
The cow hasn't got a nasty bone in her body,
from fat brown eye to foot split in two
she's a slurping awkward dome of contentment
who doesn't understand
and forgets soon after
the hot afternoon
when a woman brought them biscuits

and the cows shambled mildly into a circle,
bubbles of snot cracking from their friendly noses,
their tongues like slabs of live pink custard
investigating their nostrils, as they edged
closer and closer without interest or meaning,
blowing their grassy breath into her face,
their tails swishing away the light,
the panicky flies, the air
growing hotter and darker;
shambling off a short time later
over a strange crushed earth, wetter than flesh.

Baby

How many of us begin this way –
a scheme by one or other, a plot
to manufacture love, dreamt up
by tellers weary of their story.

Always I believed that to exist
one must be loved. Now I dream
a more wearied story, whose plot
shows the stuff I'm made of.

The baby downstairs cries. Is she
loved enough to sway the story?
She knows neither weariness nor dreams,
nor that this particular plot

was written long before she came.
She is their story's epitaph,
the end of love, its weary dream:
a plot of earth, well tended.

Blackpool Tower – New Attractions

I *The Turtles at Underwater World*

After the old Wurlitzer
big as a supermarket fridge
had drawn the white heads of the old ladies
round the shiny ballroom one last time,
we pushed to Underwater World through the screams
of unattended racing car machines
and the epileptic rolling eyes
of one-armed bandits. They crowded round us,
like beggars around apostles.

There were five turtles. They were huge,
like amoebae in a microscope,
swirling all the way to the ceiling.
To the fruit machine's *Oh My Darling Clementine!*
one did a perfect back-flip,
its dark, alien eyes very still;
soft as a foetus, or something newly skinned,
it turned on its invisible axis,
and brushed its lips against the watery roof.

Older than my dead grandfather,
older than the sum of the children
racing by to the Dinosaur Ride,
the turtles filled their tank with the rhythm
of a sea forgotten, its sounds mouthed
in the silence of the glass,
until it seemed that they were drowning,
their eyes closed, their bellies
rising and falling like moons
on a makeshift tide.

II *The Walk of Faith*

can stand the weight of five baby elephants.
I cannot do it, I cannot cross a square of glass
though you hold my hand though you
point out that I weigh less than five baby elephants.
It is not the fear of falling,
but the fear of *disobedience* –
of walking where I was not meant to walk,
of seeing people tiny vulnerable,
without civilisation or meaning.
I have no faith: I could not cross and be unchanged.
The source of my giddiness: I am a speck in the sky
and *no one remembers me*. And at the same time
I know the tiny scattered creatures
whom we observe with mild loathing
and some pity are me. They are all me,
running without direction, as if I had plummeted though
the five-baby-elephant-proof glass and had
shattered on North Shore and all the pieces
had picked themselves up and were scuttling away.
Look – that one crosses the road a little too recklessly,
is narrowly missed by a tram, is tearing away from something.
There – another has flung her arms around a man in the street,
a man whom she thought was her father,
and indeed he seems not unwilling to take on the role,
he has embraced her, he is kissing her hair,
telling her *I will try anything twice* and laughing.
But look there: a crowd has gathered,
a circle around somebody dead in the road,
it's someone whose hate has got the better of them,
someone who's gone and got themselves killed,
and somebody's sister is sprinting towards the Pleasure Beach
– I can see from here that she's not going to make it –
the crowds are gaining on her, the swoop of the big dipper
is impossibly far away –
that other place, where people fall and do not break,
I cannot reach it, no faith I know of
can get me there.

Dear Virginia Ironside

I thought my wife and I
enjoyed an excellent sex life,
but recently she informed me
that on the point of orgasm
she feels like smashing up the room
and stamping on the pieces,
she imagines breaking my teeth
and slashing the walls with broken glass,
she feels like a shark in a feeding frenzy,
as if she's drenched in blood
and no one knows her anymore.
It puts her off, she says.
We used to make love all the time,
but now she says she's afraid of something.
She lies awake all night.
Sometimes she even cries.
I want to comfort her.
I almost reach out.
But I'm afraid that if I do
something else will come out,
a deeper fury, even worse,
and I won't know who it belongs to.

Bears

About a week afterwards,
she sees the first one,
curled between the cornflakes and the ketchup.
Its eyes are tight shut, two thin lines,
its long eyelashes quivering
with each invisible breath.
It's small enough to fill two palms,
and when she checks again
it's sleeping still,
as if only the lightest breath
could wake it.

Next day, she almost hot-washes one.
There it was, alone in the drum
like a child's mitten.
Her husband says nothing.
His mouth keeps the truth tightly in.
That night she wakes to find him sleeping
with two bears curled on his chest.

Now there are nearly twenty.
She took to feeding them at midnight
and suddenly they multiplied.
A saucer of milk on the kitchen floor,
and plump shadows come to life,
tiny lumberings across the lino,
to slurp in a circle like hedgehogs.
When she curls beside them
they rest their round snouts
on every tired crook of her.

She takes to sleeping on the floor,
clinging to the warmth of them,
even when blood seeps
from the ear of the smallest,
and they start to snarl over the milk
and in her dreams all day and night
their cries come, high pitched and thin.

Kleptomaniac

There are things which you gave me:
a bundle of letters written in green,
a man's nose, a curly way of writing 'P';
and there are things which I *took*:
this unsmiling photograph,
this t-shirt, the taste of you washed out of it.

In a bright hospital
you offered your death to me.
You gave it slowly over months
then crazily, hand over fist.
You let me come when others must not come.
You let me sit beside you through the night.
This is vulnerability, the gift tag said,
your gift to me.

But of course it wasn't enough.
I couldn't stop a habit so long engrained.

On the last night, I snatched
a long look at you when we were alone.
I half-inched
a touch from your hand on my mouth
that you would never have allowed.
I lifted
your smile at the sound of my name
and I ran with it.

Like a stolen child
that all of Scotland Yard
and all the world's fathers are searching for,
I shut it in a dark place
where I wrapped it
over and over
in my delight.

Pilate Comes to My Father's Deathbed

On the last day
they summoned me, and I came to his bedside.
When I asked him, *so, you are the king*
he merely smiled. I looked to his followers.
One said, *I do not care what he has done*
and the others said nothing.

It was a difficult case.
He did not express remorse, nor love.
His only word was *discomfort*
as the nurses turned him a last time.

I looked for a sign
that there was a case to answer. It seemed
that there was, and there was not.
I heard of no tenderness, nor compassion.
But there was a framed photo
and a daughter, and a son.

I said to them, *shall I stop this?*
and they merely wept.
I said to him, *do you understand my authority?*
Speak. Justify yourself.

He said nothing
and I was decided.
When the others could not bear
to see the drop of his head,
the sweating of his skin,
the blindness of his eyes,
I took my place by his face.

And when his gasps drew no air
and his frantic heart jumped
and his hand grew icy
I did nothing.
I could see no case to answer.
I turned him over to his own people.

Progress Diary

I've tried everything else; I'll try this.
Forget yourself. It's a glossy idea. Costs a packet.
Day one: everyone's crying without actually crying.
Everyone's loveless, penniless, hopeless,
and hungry, hungry, hungry.
Comfort 2 people. Shed 0 tears.

Day two: my father's dying, disastrously slowly.
I touch the hands of people I've never met.
They've come to cry and end up crying.
Loss can be assuaged by others.
But they say my hands are cold.
Comfort 3.5 people. Shed 0 tears.

Day three: I've salvaged a pen and a camera.
I take pictures, but the cold is terrible.
There's a fog I can't see through. I talk
to anyone who'll listen, even though it's against the rules.
They turn their heads ever-so-slightly.
But I've thrown open the door and I can't stop.
The weak light bathes me in stillness.
I stuff the air with words.
I can't stop until I retch.
Comfort 0 people. Shed (approx) 3 tears.

Day five: Last night I remembered him. I heard the room say
forever. I am fuzzy headed, cold.
Comfort 0 people. Shed 0 tears.

Metamorphosis

'It happens that I'm tired of being a man.'
— PABLO NERUDA
(from 'Walking Around')

It happens that in the morning
just before I wake, when the world
lays its palms gently upon my eyes,
it happens that my cheekbones are hollow,
and a damp pallor inhabits my skin.
The final ugliness of death,
like that of the sick predator
with slow blinking eyes, I feel it enter me.
Father, I've been writing to you.
I've been touching your picture.
I've been drafting and redrafting
your certainty that it wasn't over.
You wrote on a corner of paper
don't panic. Father, it happens
that your tired skin has been delivered to me.
Someone's gathered it up in the dawn air.
Someone's wrapping it round me.
My mouth's open in a death yawn,
my fingers are heavy,
my legs thin and untouchable.
I'm struggling to wake, but it seems so far away.
I feel a flutter of pain through fog,
I turn myself with difficulty.
Father, it happens that I die like this
each dawn, each half-sleep.
Later, when I am dressed, and for all the world
a woman, I catch sight of myself in the mirror.
Death has left a trace of its ugliness.
You've etched it into me, my heritage.
Father, it happens that I'm tired with the weight of it,
the knife of your face, the stones of your hands.

Labour

The swollen woman before her
buries a shoulder in the pillow,
moans and digs slowly.
But *thank God*

the world briefly rights itself,
provides tea (whilst still chiming 13,
turning inside out, flipping over
like the belly of a slow whale).

It's eleven-twenty, and this woman
who used to be a woman like herself
is sweating and grumbling and turning into
an angel who can no longer be bothered.

A lifetime's dignity carefully accumulated
is fallen around her.
She doesn't even think of it,
the impetus to roll out from under it is irresistible.

Her male witness is quite unable to record.
He embraces his newly labouring woman,
and they move gently in this endless moment.
Once they all could touch, but now

she knows she's left them
rocking together in the wreckage of an old sea,
while another ship laboriously turns
back into a harsh oxygen.

My Faithless Mouth

It was my mouth
suddenly on the bus,
my faithless mouth
which I had sworn to silence.
My mouth, the filthy whorish thing
threw itself open on the bus
in front of all the schoolboys
and the mums on their way to the Co-op.
No sound came out,
but that was of no consequence:
the secret was out
and all the scraps of hospital
that I'd been trying to hold onto
began to worm their way out of my eyes.
My mouth, shocked at what it had begun,
tried to close itself.
It turned my head to the window
so that only the lonely wife
dusting the butterflies
nailed to the outside of her home
looked and looked away.
I coughed. I waved. I pulled out a magazine.
My mouth, in the glare of publicity,
forgot everything and slipped offstage.
I grabbed my eyes and cheeks and nose
which now were sliding down my neck
and stuffed them in my bag,
striding blankly from the bus.
I ran whimpering home.
We sat on the edge of the bed.
I could see that he was terrified.
He said, 'Don't worry. It's all right.'
as from the hole where my mouth had been
popped a plump leg, an oil slick wing.

The Writing on the Fridge

We unsnap the pieces
of our new-bought Erotic Poetry
and gigglingly announce
our *glistening apparatus,*
our *pubic joy,* our
languid moaning nipples.
But soon we're out of prepositions,
pronouns (special pack required),
something to let us know
who's doing what to whom.
Our fridge is swaggering
but ultimately inarticulate.
Show me what you want, he says
and through the hungry words I search,
like a child scanning half-familiar crowds
pouring from an unknown place.
He's watching me eagerly
as I take out the scissors –
and *snip! snip! snip!*
turn a handful of words into babble.
Through the corner of my eye
I watch his smile,
observe how it freezes,
as an unbelievable story spells itself out
one letter at a time,
uneven and frantic.